D1442103

Nocturnal Animals

Aye-Ayes

Kristin Petrie
ABDO Publishing Company

visit us at
www.abdopublishing.com

Published by ABDO Publishing Company, 8000 West 78th Street, Edina, Minnesota 55439.
Copyright © 2010 by Abdo Consulting Group, Inc. International copyrights reserved in all
countries. No part of this book may be reproduced in any form without written permission from the
publisher. The Checkerboard Library™ is a trademark and logo of ABDO Publishing Company.

Printed in the United States of America, North Mankato, Minnesota.
082009
012010

 PRINTED ON RECYCLED PAPER

Cover Photo: Photolibrary
Interior Photos: Alamy p. 18; Animals Animals p. 7; Corbis p. 19; Getty Images pp. 8, 17;
    iStockphoto pp. 12, 21; Peter Arnold p. 1; Photo Researchers p. 13; Photolibrary pp. 5, 10,
    14–15, 20

Series Coordinator: Megan M. Gunderson
Editors: Heidi M.D. Elston, Megan M. Gunderson
Art Direction & Cover Design: Neil Klinepier

Library of Congress Cataloging-in-Publication Data

Petrie, Kristin, 1970-
 Aye-ayes / Kristin Petrie.
    p. cm. -- (Nocturnal animals)
 Includes index.
 ISBN 978-1-60453-735-2
 1. Aye-aye--Juvenile literature. I. Title.
 QL737.P935P48 2010
 599.8'3--dc22

                             2009025652

Contents

Aye-Ayes

What bug-eyed animal has **rodent** teeth and elephant ears? Its long, spidery fingers help it find food at night. No, it isn't the newest video game character. This strange-sounding creature is the aye-aye.

Are you asking yourself what an aye-aye is? You are not alone! Even on its home island, the aye-aye is tough to spot. This **unique** and rare **primate** is found only in Madagascar.

The aye-aye belongs to the order Primates. This order also includes mammals such as monkeys and humans. The aye-aye is the world's largest nocturnal primate.

Nocturnal, Diurnal, or Crepuscular?

One way scientists group animals is by when they are most active. Nocturnal animals work and play during the night and sleep during the day. Diurnal animals are the opposite. They rest at night and are active during the day. Crepuscular animals are most active at twilight. This includes the time just before sunrise or just after sunset.

The aye-aye is the only species in the family **Daubentoniidae**. Its scientific name is *Daubentonia madagascariensis*. Keep reading to learn more about this bushy-tailed, long-fingered creature. Maybe you'll spot something humans have in common with this fellow primate!

Scientists use a method called scientific classification to sort organisms into groups. The basic classification system includes eight groups. In descending order, they are domain, kingdom, phylum, class, order, family, genus, and species.

Unique Look

The aye-aye is about the size of a small house cat. An adult usually weighs nearly 4.5 pounds (2 kg). Together, the length of its head and body averages 16 inches (40 cm). A long, bushy tail adds another 22 to 24 inches (55 to 60 cm).

Dark brown or black fur covers the aye-aye's body. The white tips of dark **guard hairs** fleck the dark coat. The bushy tail's unusually long hair can measure nine inches (22.5 cm)!

Large, black, bald ears stand out on the aye-aye's head. The face is short and pale. Dark circular markings surround the eyes. The aye-aye's eyes are bright yellowish orange. Unlike most **primates**, each eye has a third eyelid. This wets the eye and protects it from flying debris during eating.

The aye-aye's large hands are another **unique** feature. Its thin middle fingers are longer than the rest. Ball-and-socket joints make them extra **flexible**, like your shoulders and hips. The aye-aye uses these special fingers to find and eat food.

The aye-aye's tail more than doubles its length.

Island Home

In captivity, aye-ayes are provided with nest boxes and nesting materials.

To see aye-ayes in their natural **habitat**, you'll need to travel to Madagascar. There, aye-ayes roam rain forests, **deciduous** forests, and coastal forests. Aye-ayes even live on plantations of coconut, lychee, or other trees. These varied habitats may be hot, rainy, dry, or windy. Luckily, aye-ayes can survive in many conditions.

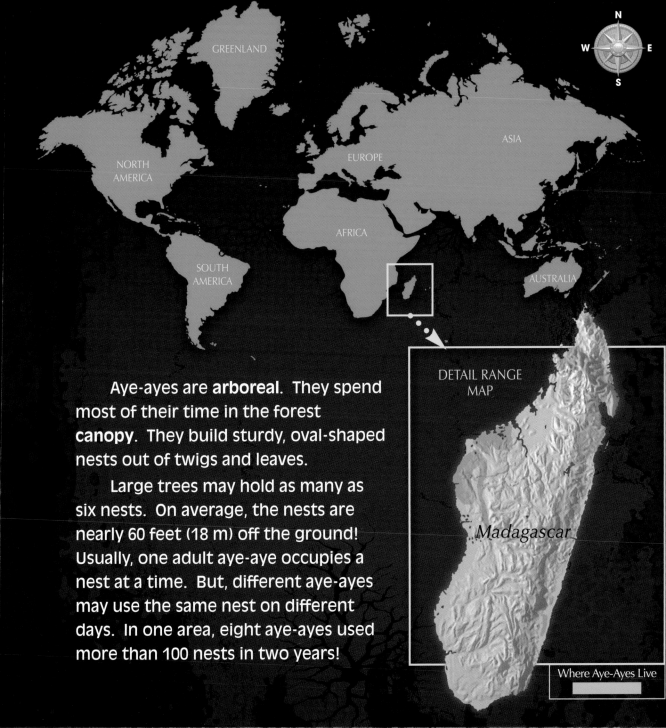

Aye-ayes are **arboreal**. They spend most of their time in the forest **canopy**. They build sturdy, oval-shaped nests out of twigs and leaves.

Large trees may hold as many as six nests. On average, the nests are nearly 60 feet (18 m) off the ground! Usually, one adult aye-aye occupies a nest at a time. But, different aye-ayes may use the same nest on different days. In one area, eight aye-ayes used more than 100 nests in two years!

N
W — E
S

GREENLAND

ASIA

EUROPE

NORTH
AMERICA

AFRICA

SOUTH
AMERICA

AUSTRALIA

DETAIL RANGE
MAP

Madagascar

Where Aye-Ayes Live

Night Vision

You have traveled to the forests of Madagascar to find an aye-aye. Once you have located a nest or two, take a nap! You will need rest to stay up all night with the aye-aye.

Since aye-ayes are nocturnal, they sleep during the day. At night, they spend time moving, eating, grooming, and resting. Like many other nocturnal animals, aye-ayes have special eye features. They help the aye-aye see better in the dark.

Young aye-ayes have green eyes.
As adults, their eyes appear orange.

Some lucky nocturnal animals have special eye features that help them in the dark. They may have large eyes compared to their body size. Also, their pupils may open wider than ours do in low light. These two features allow more light to enter their eyes.

After light enters an eye's pupil, the lens focuses it on the retina. In the retina, two special kinds of cells receive the light. These are rods and cones.

Rods work in low light. They detect size, shape, and brightness. Cones work in bright light. They detect color and details. Nocturnal animals often have many more rods than cones.

Many nocturnal eyes also have a tapetum lucidum behind the retina. The tapetum is like a mirror. Light bounces off of it and back through the retina a second time. This gives the light another chance to strike the rods. The reflected light then continues back out through the pupil. This causes the glowing eyes you may see at night!

RODS

CONES

RETINA

RETINA

TAPETUM LUCIDUM

RETINA

LENS

PUPIL

ANIMAL'S EYE (side view)

Finger Food

The aye-aye spends most of each night moving through the trees and searching for food. It is an omnivore. And, its diet changes with the seasons.

Lychees

Among the aye-aye's favorite foods are coconuts, lychees, and mangoes. The aye-aye uses a long middle finger to scoop out a fruit's fleshy insides.

The aye-aye also likes ramy nuts, which are similar to walnuts. It uses its sharp **incisors** to crack the hard shells. This wears down these long teeth, which grow continuously.

No other primate has continuously growing incisors.

The aye-aye depends on its long third finger to eat its favorite foods.

As an omnivore, the aye-aye also eats animals. One of its favorite foods is insect larvae. To find it, the aye-aye taps its long middle finger along a tree branch. It also keeps its face close to the branch.

Scientists are still studying how this behavior helps the aye-aye find food. Tapping may reveal hollow spaces or soft spots in a branch. This could indicate larvae are living inside.

Tapping may also make the larvae move. Then, the aye-aye's sensitive ears can hear them. The aye-aye may even be able to smell these tasty treats.

Once the aye-aye locates squirming larvae, it gnaws through the wood. Then, it sticks its long finger into the branch. Using it like a spoon, the aye-aye scoops out the food. Are you allowed to eat with your fingers?

The aye-aye also uses its long middle finger to drink liquids. It quickly moves the finger back and forth between the liquid and its mouth. The aye-aye can move its hand 3.3 times per second to do this!

15

Young Aye-Ayes

The aye-aye's life begins with the mating of its parents. Mating takes place year-round. The female aye-aye attracts males with a **unique** mating call.

By age three and a half, a female aye-aye can begin having young. From then on, she can reproduce once every two to three years.

The female aye-aye carries one tiny aye-aye at a time. She gives birth after 160 to 170 days. A newborn aye-aye weighs just 3.2 to 4.9 ounces (90 to 140 g).

The mother nurses and cares for her baby aye-aye. By six weeks, its floppy ears become erect. For the first two months, the young aye-aye stays close to the nest. It begins jumping, playing, and exploring by the third month.

Around two years of age, the young aye-aye becomes independent. Scientists believe the aye-aye lives an average of 20 years.

One aye-aye in captivity lived to be 23 years old.

Danger!

How does the aye-aye protect itself from predators? Simply being nocturnal is one way. Living high in the forest **canopy** also provides some safety.

The aye-aye has a single natural predator. Like the aye-aye, the catlike fossa hangs out in the forest at night. It lives in the

Aye-ayes become pests when they destroy coconut crops.

Like the aye-aye, the fossa is native to Madagascar.

trees and on the ground. The fossa preys on many small animals in Madagascar. This includes the aye-aye.

Humans are the aye-aye's main threat. Some people see the aye-aye as good luck. Yet others believe the aye-aye is a sign of evil and death. These people may kill the aye-aye on sight to prevent the bad luck.

The aye-aye's feeding habits also create conflict with humans. Aye-ayes may damage coconuts and other tasty crops. Then, the farmers may see aye-ayes as pests and kill them. In one case, aye-ayes were responsible for destroying nearly the entire coconut crop of two villages!

Today, the aye-aye also faces a challenge from deforestation. This practice destroys forests to make way for crops and development.

Deforestation decreases the aye-aye's food supply and destroys its homes. This threatens the aye-aye species, which requires large areas of land to survive. It also brings the aye-aye closer to human populations and plantations.

Aye-ayes are widespread and adapt easily. Still, scientists believe the aye-aye population is decreasing.

The aye-aye is not yet **endangered**. But it could easily become so in the near future. So, this animal requires protection.

Conservation efforts have already begun. In Madagascar, several nature reserves and national parks protect the aye-aye and its **habitat**. And, scientists study the aye-aye in the wild and in **captivity**. With increased awareness, the aye-aye will continue to thrive and amaze us.

Protecting Madagascar's varied habitats will help the aye-aye survive.

Glossary

arboreal (ahr-BAWR-ee-uhl) - living in or frequenting trees.

canopy - the uppermost spreading, branchy layer of a forest.

captivity - the state of being captured and held against one's will.

conservation - the planned management of natural resources to protect them from damage or destruction.

Daubentoniidae (doh-buhn-toh-NEYE-uh-dee) - the scientific name for the aye-aye family. The aye-aye is the only species in its family.

deciduous (dih-SIH-juh-wuhs) - shedding leaves each year. Deciduous forests have trees or shrubs that do this.

endangered - in danger of becoming extinct.

flexible - able to bend or move easily.

guard hair - one of the long, coarse hairs that protects a mammal's undercoat.

habitat - a place where a living thing is naturally found.

incisor (ihn-SEYE-zuhr) - a front tooth, usually adapted for cutting.

primate - any mammal belonging to the order Primates. Primates share features such as grasping hands or feet. Humans, monkeys, apes, and lemurs are primates.

rodent - any of several related animals that have large front teeth for gnawing. Common rodents include mice, squirrels, and beavers.

unique - being the only one of its kind.

Web Sites

To learn more about aye-ayes, visit ABDO Publishing Company on the World Wide Web at **www.abdopublishing.com**. Web sites about aye-ayes are featured on our Book Links page. These links are routinely monitored and updated to provide the most current information available.

Index